Sheep Sleep

by Pearl Markovics

Consultant:
Beth Gambro
Reading Specialist
Yorkville, Illinois

Contents

BEARPORT
PUBLISHING

New York, New York

Sheep Sleep

Let's rhyme!

Here is a **jeep**.

The mud is **deep**.

The hill is **steep.**

The **jeep** goes *beep*.

In the road are **sheep**.

The **sheep** are fast **asleep**.

Beep, beep.
Wake up, **sheep**!

Key Words in the **-eep** Family

asleep

deep

jeep

sheep

steep

Other **-eep** Words:
creep, keep, seep, weep

Index

About the Author

Pearl Markovics enjoys having fun with words. She especially likes witty wordplay.

Teaching Tips

Before Reading

✔ Introduce rhyming words and the **-eep** word family to readers.

✔ Guide readers on a "picture walk" through the text by asking them to name the things shown.

✔ Discuss book structure by showing children where text will appear consistently on pages. Highlight the supportive pattern of the book.

During Reading

✔ Encourage readers to "read with your finger" and point to each word as it is read. Stop periodically to ask children to point to a specific word in the text.

✔ Reading strategies: When encountering unknown words, prompt readers with encouraging cues such as:

- **Does that word look like a word you already know?**
- **Does it rhyme with another word you have already read?**

After Reading

✔ Write the key words on index cards.

- **Have readers match them to pictures in the book.**

✔ Ask readers to identify their favorite page in the book. Have them read that page aloud.

✔ Choose an **-eep** word. Ask children to pick a word that rhymes with it.

✔ Ask children to create their own rhymes using **-eep** words. Encourage them to use the same pattern found in the book.

Credits: Cover, © RasaSopittakamol/Shutterstock, © PinkBlue/Shutterstock, and © Sylvie Bouchard/Shutterstock; 2–3, © garett_mosher/iStock; 4–5, © MousePotato/iStock; 6–7, © MousePotato/iStock; 8–9, © elbobinho/Shutterstock; 10–11, © MousePotato/iStock and © Gabriele Ritz/Shutterstock; 12–13, © MousePotato/iStock; 14–15, © Eric Isselee/Shutterstock and © garett_mosher/iStock; 16T (L to R), © borchee/iStock, © MousePotato/iStock, and © garett_mosher/iStock; 16B (L to R), © Eric Isselee/Shutterstock and © MousePotato/iStock.

Publisher: Kenn Goin **Senior Editor**: Joyce Tavolacci **Creative Director**: Spencer Brinker

Library of Congress Cataloging-in-Publication Data: Names: Markovics, Pearl, author. | Gambro, Beth, consultant. Title: Sheep sleep / by Pearl Markovics; consultant: Beth Gambro, Reading Specialist, Yorkville, Illinois. Description: New York, New York: Bearport Publishing, [2020] | Series: Read and rhyme: Level 2 | Includes index. Identifiers: LCCN 2019007620 (print) | LCCN 2019012644 (ebook) | ISBN 9781642806021 (ebook) | ISBN 9781642805482 (library) | ISBN 9781642807141 (pbk.) Subjects: LCSH: Readers (Primary) Classification: LCC PE1119 (ebook) | LCC PE1119 .M28586 2020 (print) | DDC 428.6/2–dc23 LC record available at https://lccn.loc.gov/2019007620

10 9 8 7 6 5 4 3 2 1